A STROLL THROUGH OLD MUMBLES

Views from my Postcard Collection

KEN REEVES

Sou'wester Books

For Mollie, my dear wife.

First impression   1992

Second printing   1999

Copyright   ©   Ken Reeves / Sou'wester Books   1992 and 1999

ISBN   0 9515281 3 0

Published by Sou'wester Books, 25 Kelvinbrook, West Molesey, Surrey. KT8 1RU

Printed by Brynymor, Darcy Business Centre, Llandarcy, Neath. SA10 6EJ Tel: 01792 326300

INTRODUCTION

Following the success of his first book "A Stroll Through Old Swansea", Ken Reeves has now selected the best views of Mumbles from his extensive collection of old postcards.

This selection covers the original parish of Oystermouth (the whole area being generally referred to as Mumbles) from Blackpill to Caswell.

The postcards were all published before the 1930s and the majority date from the earliest years of the century. The cards are the work of many publishers both national and local. As Mumbles had its own publisher, Melville Clare, a number of his views are reproduced here.

If picture postcards of West Cross and Norton were ever produced they do not appear in this collection as the author has been unable to find any.

That Mumbles was a place of recreation is evident in these lovely photographs. Thousands of visitors arrived each summer day on the Mumbles railway, to stroll around the cliffs, walk along the pier or sit (in their best clothes) on the beach.

But this is a picture book and, apart from a few words of explanation, we must let the postcards speak for themselves.

The 'Roman' Bridge at Blackpill looks at its best with this group of Edwardian children.

Thatched cottages in Mill Lane, Blackpill. (M.A. Clare)

The lodge at Clyne Castle.

On the Mumbles Road at Lilliput between Blackpill and West Cross.

This view of Norton was taken from the battlements of Oystermouth Castle.
(J.B.W.S.)

Taken from the field where Castle Crescent now stands this view dates from the early 1890s before the railway was extended to Southend and the beach reclaimed. On the right is the White Rose public house, and on the corner of the Dunns the Oystermouth Coffee Tavern. Across the road is J. Eley, family butcher.

A STROLL THROUGH OLD MUMBLES

10   A STROLL THROUGH OLD MUMBLES

Clement's Quarry is now a car park. On the far side of the main road are the buildings of John Jones Mumbles Dairy and The Elms both now demolished and also a car park.

This card is captioned 'Mumbles Cabbies Fishing Club, 1909' and refers to the cabbies whips. They are waiting in the station square at Oystermouth for passengers arriving by the Mumbles train.
(M.A. Clare)

12   A STROLL THROUGH OLD MUMBLES

This general view of the village shows that the area reclaimed from the sea is already built over. As well as the terraces which are familiar to us a magnifying glass will reveal the Kursaal (now the Tivoli), the figure eight railway (now the tennis courts and bowling green), and Tom Owen's pavilion (now Our Lady Star of the Sea). (Royal Photographic Co.)

Taken from Colts Hill this view of the village shows the top of the lime kiln to the left and the roof of Oystermouth school beyond.
(M.A. Clare)

A STROLL THROUGH OLD MUMBLES

Oystermouth Castle. This photograph was taken from the field where Castle Avenue now stands. (Royal Photographic Co.)

14   A STROLL THROUGH OLD MUMBLES

*Ivy clad Oystermouth Castle.
(Wrench series)*

The Parish Hall and National School was opened in 1908. Many village children will remember their days there when it was Mumbles Junior Mixed. (M.A. Clare)

The crowded graves at Oystermouth Church told us much of the village's past but have largely been removed. (Royal Photographic Co.)

A STROLL THROUGH OLD MUMBLES **17**

The interior of All Saints Church, Oystermouth at the turn of the century.
(Zenith)

Members of Oystermouth Urban District Council take the inaugural trip on the figure eight railway. This was built on part of the 'ballast bank' which had been enclosed by the railway extension. The figure eight was later moved to Victoria Park, Swansea, and is now at Porthcawl. (M.A. Clare)

Who would guess that this is Woodville Road? (Stewart & Woolf)

Local people called this Taylor's Corner after the grocer's shop. Beyond the Wesleyan Church, cottages and part of Claremont Villas have now been demolished to build the Post Office and shops.
(Zenith)

A STROLL THROUGH OLD MUMBLES   21

The Dunns. This is the reverse of the last view. On the right is Lowther's Mumbles Pharmacy now occupied by Boots. Beyond is Jenkins the ironmonger which later became Forte's Ice Cream Parlour, and the buildings cleared away to widen the road.
(Valentine)

Tom Owen's Pierrotts. This concert party entertained visitors at the pavilion which became the Catholic Church.
(M.A. Clare)

Parade Gardens and Promenade Terrace on the left of the picture were built on the land reclaimed from the sea. (Valentine)

Oyster skiffs inside the breakwater at what is now the Village Lane slipway. This spot was always known as 'the piles'. The skiff with the shed on its deck was naturally called the Ark and used as a workshop. (Alfred Way)

Bucket and spade at the ready this child is ready to enjoy a day on the beach. It is 1920 and the couple sit at what remains of the wooden breakwater built in the 1890s to provide a lay-up for the oyster boats after the natural lay-up was reclaimed.
(M.A. Clare)

Melville Clare took this view from behind Village Lane. Tom Owen's new pavilion became the Catholic Church. To the left one can just make out the top of the figure eight railway and beyond it the roof of the cinema. Beyond Oystermouth station is the house known as the Elms now cleared for a car park.

A STROLL THROUGH OLD MUMBLES

Melville Clare took many of the photographs that illustrate this book and published them as postcards. Here is his shop on Mumbles Road. It was more recently Smale's the greengrocer, an antique shop and now the Mumbles General Trading Co.
(M.A. Clare)

28 A STROLL THROUGH OLD MUMBLES

The Bridgwater ketch Jane moored off the promenade at Southend.
(M. A. Clare)

A STROLL THROUGH OLD MUMBLES

30   A STROLL THROUGH OLD MUMBLES

Southend. The Ship & Castle public house on the right is now the Conservative Club. Further along the road is the Mermaid Hotel and next Beaufort Buildings which included a dairy, the Gladstone Oyster & Coffee Tavern and Southend Sub Post Office.
(Royal Photographic Co.)

Southend. The Mermaid Hotel, the London Dining Rooms and the Ship & Castle Inn.

The George Hotel. A little girl plays with the pump. (M.A. Clare)

The Bristol Channel Yacht Club. In the wall between the lamp post and the club house is the Lifeboat barometer which dates from 1866 and is now in the lifeboat house. (Valentine)

A STROLL THROUGH OLD MUMBLES

Southend and Oystermouth taken from the Knab a few years before the railway was extended to the Pier. Oyster skiffs are on the moorings.

Regatta Day in about 1902. The lifeboat has been manouvered onto its carriage for rehousing. This slipway is now used to launch the inshore lifeboat and boats of Mumbles Rowing Club.
(B. Parry, Swansea)

36 A STROLL THROUGH OLD MUMBLES

The Cutting was made in 1887 to allow the main road to continue to Bracelet and Limeslade. (Valentine)

This view was taken before the building of the pier or the extension of the railway. The oyster skiffs are on their moorings.
(Valentine)

A STROLL THROUGH OLD MUMBLES 37

38   A STROLL THROUGH OLD MUMBLES

Capt. Twomey, the Pier Master, at the Winter Gardens which stood in front of the Pier Hotel.

An unusual shot of the pier taken from the cliff above the Pier Hotel. One of Campbell's White Funnel paddle steamers (it looks like the Ravenswood) arriving.

A STROLL THROUGH OLD MUMBLES

Mumbles Head from the Pier.

40 A STROLL THROUGH OLD MUMBLES

A stroll along the pier was an essential part of the Edwardian's visit to the seaside.

The crowd on Mumbles Pier is entertained by the band while it waits for the paddle steamer. (Valentine)

Crowds arrived at the Pier aboard the Mumbles train to catch a paddle steamer for Ilfracombe. (Valentine)

This view of Mumbles Pier was taken in 1929 when the electric tramcars had replaced the steam trains.

A STROLL THROUGH OLD MUMBLES 43

Natural Arch, Mumbles.

44 A STROLL THROUGH OLD MUMBLES

The lighthouse seen through the natural arch which stood for centuries on the middle island. The arch came down in a storm in December 1910.

Swimming, paddling and boat trips at Bracelet Bay.

Limeslade Bay, Mumbles

46 A STROLL THROUGH OLD MUMBLES

Sunbathing was not the done thing in the days before the 1914-18 war. Sitting on the pebbles or taking a boat trip were the only amusements at Limeslade.
(Zenith)

LIMESLADE BUNGALOWS.

The bungalows at Plunch Lane, Limeslade, have largely been replaced by their modern equivalent.

A STROLL THROUGH OLD MUMBLES 47

The coastguard officer puts the Mumbles Life-Saving Apparatus Company through a practice drill in 1919. The breeches buoy as it was popularly known was used to rescue the crews of ships wrecked close in-shore. (M.A. Clare)

48 A STROLL THROUGH OLD MUMBLES

The White Lady. This ship's figure-head stood in the garden of Lewin's Hill at Thistleboon. (W.H. Smith)

A STROLL THROUGH OLD MUMBLES

Oystermouth Cemetery was opened in the 1880s and is seen here about 1905.
(Harvey Barton, Bristol)

Newton. This view dates from 1900 and is taken from the junction of Nottage Road, Southward Lane and Newton Road.

Newton in the early years of the century. This is the junction of Newton Road and New Well Lane. The Post Office is yet to be built.

St Peter's Church, Newton, soon after its consecration in 1903.
(Alfred Way, Swansea)

'Sunshine Corner'. The Children's Special Service Mission at Rotherslade, August 1917. (M.A. Clare)

This postcard was captioned 'Langland Cove' otherwise known as Little Langland or Ladies Bay. Today we know it as Rotherslade.
(Alfred Way)

56 A STROLL THROUGH OLD MUMBLES

Access to the beach at Rotherslade was provided by rickety wooden steps. The cliff path above the bay was supported by timber. These were replaced by the concrete shelter which local people call the 'White Elephant'.

Langland Bay.
(Valentine)

This turn of the century view of Langland shows the hotel, originally the country home of the Crawshay family of Merthyr. For years it was known as the Convalescent or Miners' Home.
(Harvey Barton, Bristol)

58   A STROLL THROUGH OLD MUMBLES

An unusual view of Langland allows us a peep into the coach yard of the Langland Bay Hotel and gardens. (Stengel & Co. London)

This view of Caswell shows the remains of the windmill in the distance and, on the right, the pumping station which replaced it to pump water from Redlay spring to the reservoir in Newton.
(Valentine)

60 A STROLL THROUGH OLD MUMBLES